RESEARCH PROPOSAL
Contents & Exemplars

Professor Javed Iqbal Saani, PhD

Intellectual Capital Enterprise Limited, London

Published by Intellectual Capital Enterprise Limited, ICE Kemp House, 152-160 City Road London, EC1 V2N
Printed in England

CONTENTS

DEDICATION

To my parents who invested heavily for our education and remained engaged in prayers for our success and good being

ACKNOWLEDGEMENT

Special gratitude is due to all those who helped me to compile the work. The contribution of my colleague Muhammad Nadeem Khan who was the co-author in one of my previous books for the first exemplar of the present volume is worthwhile.

I am also obliged to my family who spared me to embark on the project. They also provide valuable information which enriched the contents of this effort. May Allah reward them for their contribution? Ameen!

Once I sent an article to the editor of a journal he said there is plethora of material already published so what is the reason I should publish your article. I replied I have arranged the material in a novice way which may be the only reason for its eligibility to be published. It is an established fact that a theory can be corroborated with a different research method, data set, respondents, settings etc. It inspired me to start the project; I had written many research proposals for many occasions. For instance, for the guidance of students, post doc submission, for a publisher for one of my books etc. I thought it may be good for others who are entering the field of research or want to enhance their understanding of the phenomenon. When I entered in the area I have undergone many issues and difficulties to understand the matter.

The proposals contain popular themes such as introduction, research, question, objectives, literature review, method, scope, analysis strategy, and possible outcome. Each of the sample proposals that follow discuss these elements; they are tailored with the title. The readers can take them as exemplars to design their required proposals.

Suggestions are welcome so that they may be incorporated in the future editions.

Javed Iqbal Saani, Ph. D

Manchester August 15 2016

1 INTRODUCTION: THE CONTENTS

INTRODUCTION

One of my research papers was getting good acceptance in the academic circles and elsewhere which was based upon the first chapter of my doctoral thesis. It was linked with my research proposal submitted for the same qualification. Many academic institutions and practitioners included the research paper in their reference list for writing research proposals at various levels of academic achievements. Some of these include:

1-The Deakin University Australia. It ranked the article as an excellent piece of work on the subject (Exhibit A1 and A2).

2-DeVilgo University in the sources of information (Exhibit A3)

3-Report of five Universities of Lithuania (Exhibit A4)

4-Lovely University in its recommended list of compulsory reading (Exhibit A5)

5-Singapore Management University in its list of sources for dissertation/thesis research and writing articles (Exhibit A6)

6-Proceeding of a Sri Lankan University (Exhibit A7)

8-Google documents (Exhibit A8)

9-Handbook of Research (Exhibit A9)

10-Military Leadership, a book (Exhibit A10)

11-Scribd (Exhibit A11)

12-CiteSeerX (Exhibit A12)

13-ISM in its list of references (Exhibit A13)

14-An article in numeristic theory (Exhibit A14)

15- Mediterranean Journal of Social Sciences in the reference list of its articles (Exhibit A15)

In addition, many other researchers referred it since its appearance on the literature. Most of the researchers have used the concepts of the article for compiling their proposals that follow. It is believed that these documents may be beneficial for the research community at large. So they are put together here in the form of the booklet.

The paper consists of four parts: context (researchers' background), contents (research question (RQ) / statement of the problem, research objectives, importance of the study, philosophical assumptions, and scope of research), process (research method and the conceptual framework) and product (the outcome of the study). And usual 'front bits' i.e. introduction, literature review.

Some elements such as philosophical assumptions are desired in doctoral research in order to introduce the world view of the researcher. However, most of other components can be included in any research proposal. Again it depends upon the requirements of the audience and resources available to the researcher.

The key elements of the article are summarized in the following paragraphs for a quick look at the contents.

THE CONTEXT

The context includes the professional background of the researcher. It is important to identify the topic of research for the researcher; the evaluation team (individual) can understand the journey of the candidate. The team members can find the reasons for appropriateness of the researcher for the topic. For instance, researcher's educational background, work experience, training received and culture from which he belongs gives clue to them. A candidate from computer science may not be appropriate for a topic of economics. However, if he has received training in any particular aspect of economics than the team can consider him for the topic.

I met a marketing analyst who was working in a development bank which were identifying development projects in underdevelopment areas of a country. The bank was preparing feasibility studies for the new projects. The guy was doing market analysis for the feasibilities. He had earned a master degree in history but received short training in market analysis. My teacher in the university of Hull, department of Management Sciences and Systems was teaching systems development but his terminal degree was in physics. C. K. Prahalad was one of the guru/thinker of management but his first degree was in physics as well. There are hundreds of such examples where people changed their primary subjects and earned name in other fields. However, the transformation always linked with some event (s). The evaluation team can analyze the background and the process through which it had happened. Iqbal (2007) changed his quantitative perspective to qualitative paradigm after teaching such courses.

In addition, employment, previous projects, personal choice, and cultural background also play important role in the selection of a topic. Personality type is important; there are two types of personalities in general: introvert and extrovert. The former tends towards working alone while the latter is keen go outside and meet new people. So he is good for marketing type topics and the former for accounting and computing topics. Bryman (2001) referred examples of people who had a given interest in a subject such as Zukin's interest in loft living and his own in Disney. In short, the researcher has to associate his professional background with their topics. I used to suggest my MPhil students to enhance their dissertations in their pursuit to doctoral studies.

CONTENTS

Contents are the core of the proposal. Research question, research objective, philosophical assumptions, scope, and importance of the topic are key elements.

Research Objectives (RO)

There is a convention of starting research with research question but I think the objectives should be the starting point because these are the targets to achieve through the research project. The experience teaches that the arrangement should be changed because the research question (RQ) is a one sentence summary of these objectives.

It is recommended that there should be more than one objective because the researcher needs to understand or know the phenomenon and to develop its relationship with another factor. Knowing is not enough especially at doctoral level where addition to knowledge is desirable. Philip and Pugh (1994) define newness as "making a synthesis that hasn't been made before; using already known material but with a new interpretation, bringing new evidence to bear on an old issue." It is also part of it that a researcher does the same with a new research method. For instance, if these elements were identified with a survey and another researcher tries to replicate them with a case study.

RO define the potential achievements at one hand and provide focus on the other hand in order to collect right data. Brexit is a hot question these days. A researcher can find its impacts on employment say over the next decade (2017-2026). His recommended RO (s) may be

1-To understand the meaning of Brexit at large

2-To measure the variations in employment (increase or decrease)

3-To quantify them in monetary terms (wages, taxes etc.)

There are numerous aspects of Brexit i.e. human, movement, changes in employment, changes in frequency of travel, changes in prices, demand of housing etc. Secondly, there will be some changes in employment because the exchange of employees to and from the continent Europe. Thirdly they would effect on the wages; it is believed that European labour was cheaper than the locals. It implies that wages would go up.

The above discussion suggests that the objectives have been arranged in a logical sequence and there is a relationship between at least two of them.

They provide the focus. The first objective is a broad term which means different phenomenon for different people or stakeholders. It suggests something to politicians but not the same thing economic planners. There are other economic or related aspects but the researcher narrows down it in the second objective when he takes out employment only for his research project. The third objective fine tunes further by concentrating on wages and taxes i.e. monetary effects. He could consider other aspects as well e.g. social impacts, behavioral effects, habits of people, working pattern etc.

The researcher should define objectives carefully by understanding the subject matter and its scope, pros, and cons. Review of literature is a good way to understand the topic.

Research question (RQ)

It summarizes the theme of the work and provides the road map to be followed. Baker (2000) argues that RQ defines the problem or issue to delineate the project from others and clarify the idea. It should be precise and clear.

A good RQ can offer many messages to the readers. The wording informs the research method to be employed. For instance, word 'learning', 'understanding' etc signify that the study is using qualitative approach for data collection and analysis. The word 'perception' indicates that the study applies a survey. Iqbal and Yaqoob (2014) applied survey to measure the perception of customer.

RQ also shows the scope of research. Consider the following question.

What are the impacts of Brexit on employment in the United Kingdom from 2017 to 2021?

Brexit, employment, United Kingdom and 2017 to 2021 limits the study in a time framework (2017 to 2012), in a geographical area (United Kingdom), in a given sub-topic (employment) and the main topic (Brexit). The researcher need to articulate RQ taking into account these factors. It makes easy to limit the amount of data and its jurisdiction. Thus, it saves efforts and time which may be devoted to other aspects.

RQ can demonstrate the application of specific research method. Consider the following research question.

What are learnings from the middle management practices in Pakistan Telecommunication Company Limited (PTCL)?

The research method is explicit; PTCL is an organization and the 'learning' was gained in it. Learning indicates a qualitative approach and PTCL shows it is achieved in an organization. Thus, it implies the research method must be a case study. However, other possibilities and option are there to address the same or similar RQ.

While articulating a RQ the researcher must consider that it should be interesting to gain the attention of the reader; never been researched in the same context. It is recommended that it will produce significant outcome; able to trigger further research in the field or related areas. The researcher can make it within time and resource constraints (Wyatt and Guly, 2002). It should be theory testing or theory making and grounded in the literature so that links can be developed in the existing repository of knowledge.

Hulley et al (2007) believe that a RQ should be feasible (adequate number of subjects, adequate technical expertise, affordable in time and money, manageable in scope), novel (confirms, refutes or extends previous findings, provides new findings), ethical (amenable to a study that is relevant norms of the society at large), and relevant (to scientific knowledge, and to future research).

Finally, the number of research question in a proposal. Although more than one research question can be addressed but it is appropriate for experienced researchers. In extreme circumstances, a novice can design multiple questions depending upon the nature of research but one should consider only a single one. It is because multiple question need many streams of analysis. Sometimes requires more than one data collection and analysis strategies. It makes things complicated especially for novice who are in the process of learning and it is enough for them to make things simple.

Scope

Purpose of scope is to define the limits of the research. It guides to collect 'right' and enough data. It also provides focus which a must in advanced research and formal research programs such as research papers and doctoral studies.

Scope can be determined in a number of ways. Time-oriented: a bracket of time is selected for data instances e.g. one year, five years or a decade etc. It should be enough for a given project; a doctoral team requires five or more instances or years. Some organization publish data (statistics) biannually. So data for ten years will be required for a doctoral thesis.

Geographical area: a country, group of countries, a state/province, district etc can be taken. It implies data will be collected from this particular area only. Organization: an organization, division (s), department (s), or cost center (s) is also suitable to limit the boundaries. Also, levels of management such as top management, middle management or operational level are appropriate. Respondents: like managers, students, male, female, teenagers, professionals (any). Age: young, middle age, and old age. Income level: low, medium high, and elite is common in marketing and economics topics. In short, any one or a combination of them can be selected.

Philosophical assumptions

There are principally two paradigms that govern the philosophy of knowledge: positivistic and interpretive. The former assumes that reality is given (exists) and needs to be discovered such as H_2O was there but the researchers found it. The researchers look at an object (or issue) objectively as an indifferent observer. The outcome is quantified and expressed mathematically.

The later assumes that the reality is socially constructed; it is what people believe about a phenomenon. They express it through language, actions, and mental models. The job of a researcher is to interpret it according to his mental model and context within which anything happens. The outcome of a research project is to create an understanding or learning at the end of a research process.

While working on a proposal the researchers think about the alternatives or a combination of them. The choice leads towards the research method, data collection, and analysis strategy. The potential outcome can also be imagined at this stage. For instance, a survey is more suitable for a positivistic assumption, the data is collected through a questionnaire and analysis is through computer packages such as SPSS. It provides the numerical results which become the basis for drawing conclusion.

On the competing side, an interpretive assumption demands a case study; the data collection through interviews and observations is suitable. The data are processed with contents analysis which creates a broad picture of the matter under discussion. The researcher interprets it as 'good', 'better' 'excellent'; 'low', 'high', 'medium' etc. Any other non-numeric expression is acceptable to show the grades or ranking.

Importance of the topic

Although the project is important for the writer because he has to accomplish his studies or win a bid/funding. But it is not sufficient for the research; he has to tell the evaluation team its significance. The sponsor, the academic community, the organization where the case study may be conducted and the society at large.

When we talk about contribution to knowledge it includes all the above stakeholders. Should the project offer an addition to knowledge and the way is important for the parties concerned.

Common arguments in support of importance range from the newness of the topic to fulfill academic requirements. First, it enhances the learning of the researcher because at the end of the project he would equip himself with the knowledge and skills of a researcher. It is also helpful for his advancement in the career ladder.

Second, the research can generate a new theory or piece of knowledge which is helpful for the humanity such as a new treatment of cancer. Research in economics identified concepts and theories which are being applied in the management of economy. It is useful for economic development and general wellbeing of the society.

The academic institute where the project takes place also benefit out of the research. Big names in the industry are partly renowned for their research activities. It is also useful for their ranking which brings funding and recruitment of students.

Sometimes a topic is in practice or burning question in the research arena; any new piece of research strengthened the topic.

PROCESS

It is the way data are collected, analyzed and the broad model with the help of which conclusions will be drawn. Process includes two elements which are discussed below.

Research method

They can be broadly fall into two categories: inductive and deductive. The former is helping to create theories while the latter is used for testing theories. Social sciences apply the inductive while natural sciences employ the deductive approach. According to Trochim (2006) in the words of Soiferman (2010) "induction as moving from the specific to the general, while deduction begins with the general and ends with the specific; arguments based on experience or observation are best expressed inductively, while arguments based on laws, rules, or other widely accepted principles are best expressed deductively."

Iqbal (2007) explains the inductive as "The inductive approach on the other extreme of the pendulum draws on the hit and trail strategy. Many social situations/instances are observed, recorded or documented to extract a summary of what has been perceived. The purpose of the approach is to take out the findings from the frequent, dominant or significant themes (Thomas, 2003). He developed a general inductive approach (GIA) and purpose of this approach is to develop or establish clear links between the research objectives ... The role, experience, and knowledge of the researcher determines the nature of outcome."

Kesten and Pnueli (2005) explain the deductive method as "in the deductive method we present a small set of proof rules and show that this set is sound and relatively complete for verifying universal and existential basic assertional properties over reactive systems."

Given these broad approaches, a specific method is required. Case study, survey, laboratory experiment, field experiment, theorem proof, forecasting, and simulation are considered as scientific methods while subjective/argumentative, review, action research, descriptive/interpretive, future research and role/game playing are known as interpretive approaches (Galliers, 1992).

Research method should be linked with research objectives and research question (s). The researcher has to argue the suitability of his method to find out the answer of his question and achievement of objectives.

The conceptual framework

It is appropriate at advanced level of research but it is a positive sign if defined at less formal endeavours. It tells the reader the nature of relationship between the research project and theoretical foundations. If a theory is being tested, then arguments have to be developed how it is related with the research. For example, Iqbal (2003) has applied the framework of Pettigrew et al's (1989) in his doctoral project. It states that a change initiative consists of three stages: context, contents, and process.

A linear relationship exists in the Brexit example as discussed above among Brexit, economic impacts and employment. In some cases, it is described as a set of variables (independent and dependent) to depict the relationship that exist among them. It is augmented with moderating and mediating elements that play a role in creating outcome.

Iqbal (2007) suggests four questions in order to develop a conceptual framework:

❑ What is the broad subject involved?

❑ What is the theoretical support from the existing repository of knowledge for the subject matter?

❑ How are they linked with each other?

❑ How will the researcher apply them to conduct the present study?

Some researchers examine a phenomenon in the perspective of a particular theory. For instance, resource based view (RBV) is a managerial theory for getting competitive advantage in the industry. They need to relate their work with RBV; their conclusion should mirror the essence of the theory.

Literature review

Review of current literature is helpful to know about the topic. The purpose of review is to survey the area of knowledge and its developments over years. What criticism was made on the theories and concepts? It is recommendable that at least seven experts in the field should be surveyed; what is their work and how it is related with your research.

One way to do it is to describe the classical work from a to z in a summarized manner providing appropriate criticism. An evaluative strategy is desirable. For instance, working on Business Process Reengineering (BPR) requires that when it was introduced in the managerial arena. Who are the presenters, what was their renowned work, how it is related with the work of the research (your work)? How does it evolve since its birth?

As an example, BPR was appeared in early nineties as Business Process Redesign (Reengineering); evolved to Business Process Management by the turn of the century and faded away from the management literature gradually. Michael Hammer and Devonport were early proponents. The idea was to adopt a process view of the firm and apply technology to address emerging and existing business issues. Work force need empowerment and manager need to change their mindset from 'boss' to couch. It has been criticized on the ground that it sheds off many people which increases unemployment. However, its benefits are more than disadvantages, therefore, organizations should initiate BPR programs.

The core of review is to update readers about the subject and put forward a critical analysis of it in order to bring forward the pros and cons. A concluding view from the researcher in the form of evaluation is adding to the knowledge.

It is also a channel to justify the selected topic by relating it with the repository of existing knowledge. The researcher argues that he is not plucking in the air rather his subject is well grounded in the literature which need further work. He identifies the 'gap' in the knowledge and put forward the argument by which his work fills it. It implies the researcher is justifying the objective and the research method he is applying to achieve them.

In short, it shows the glimpses of the topic where important work is emphasized and prominent work is summarized.

THE PRODUCT

The final bit is to imagine the potential outcome of the research. Although the actual results might be different from the 'planned' yet a picture may be painted so that refinements can be made later on when the research process will complete. Product can take many dimensions.

The first outcome usually is a document in the form of a dissertation report. Technically the document should be publishable in case of a doctoral thesis. The researcher receives approval of experts to practice research. So, personal learning was the tangible outcome; he can conduct research without supervision. The skills are transferable; therefore, he can teach to others.

Second, the research should contribute to knowledge.: a synthesis, addition, confirmation, refusal, and production of new evidences about a theoretical or applied problem. The outcome will be a reference work for the research community which is itself an addition to knowledge.

Third, the research must offer something for public or society at large. Sponsors, the settings (if it is an organization), the educational institute are also expecting something.

Applied research requires that a given problem was addressed and at least some suggestions must be there for the solution of the issue.

Iqbal argues that in connection with doctoral research project that "The researcher's job is to find out:

☐ What is the theoretical contribution in the discipline concerned?

What is the practical role in solving the problem?

 How it enhances the personal and professional development of the researcher?"

An acceptable combination is desirable despite the fact that achieving a single item is enough. Whetten (1989) suggests a way forward for developing theories and thus making significant contribution to knowledge.

REFERENCES

Baker, M.J. 2000. Writing a Research Proposal, The Marketing Review, I (1), 61-75.

Bryman, Alan 2001. Social research methods, Oxford: Oxford University Press.

Galliers, R. D. 1992. Choosing IS Research Approaches, London: Blackwell Scientific Publications.

Hulley, Stephen B.; Cummings, Steven R.; Browner, Warren S.; Grady, Deborah G.; Newman, Thomas B. 2007. Designing Clinical Research, 3rd Edition, Philadelphia: Lippincott Williams & Wilkins.

Iqbal, J. 2003. Learning from the radical change initiative in British aerospace military aircraft, thesis (Ph.D.). Salford University.

Iqbal, J. 2007. Learning from a doctoral research project: structure and content of a research proposal, European Journal of Business Research Methods, 5(1), 11-20.

Iqbal, Javed and Samina Yaqoob 2014. Perceptions of customer about the service quality in one-stop-shops of Pakistan Telecommunication Company Limited (PTCL) and their implications for management, European Journal of Scientific Research, 127(3), 238-249.

Kesten, Yonit and Pnueli Amir 2005. A compositional approach to CTL* verification, Theoretical Computer Science, 331(2-3), 397-428.

Pettigrew, A.M., R. Whipp and R. Rosenfeld, 1989. Competitiveness and the management of strategic change, In Arthur, Francis and Tharakan, P. K. M. ed. The competitiveness of European industry, London: Routledge.

Pkillips, E, and Pugh, D. 1994. How to Get a Ph.D., Buckingham: Open University Press.

Soiferman, L. Karen 2010. Compare and Contrast Inductive and Deductive Research Approaches, Working Paper University of Manitoba.

Thomas, D R 2003. A general inductive approach for qualitative data analysis, School of Population Health, Working Paper University of Auckland.

Trochim, W.M.K. 2006. Research methods knowledge base. Retrieved on January 25, 2010, from http://www.socialresearchmethods.net

Whetten, David A. 1989. What Constitutes a Theoretical Contribution? Academy of Management Review, 14(4), 490–495.

Wyatt, J. and Guly H 2002. Identifying the research question and planning the project, The Emergency Medicine Journal, 19(3), 18-321.

2 PROJECT PLANNING IN THE CONTEMPORARY BUSINESS ENVIRONMENT[1]

Introduction

Juran (1989) views a project as a schedule for solution. A schedule defines the activities and corresponding time of doing that activity, starting or finishing. This view assumes timing dimension. However, a project is more than that and normally includes many other elements. Andersen (1995) and his colleagues believe a project is a combination of a unique task, is designated to achieve a specific result, requires a variety of resources, and limited in time. A project's uniqueness separates it from routine work and other projects being undertaken in an organization. For example, development of a website for a university is a specific and on-off job. It is developed under copy write laws or its patent rights might be the property of a separate organization than the website developer. A project is also meant to achieve one or more objectives; it

---

[1] Initially written for a master dissertation.

may be an artifact, efficiency, profitability or customer satisfaction. All that need resources: human, financial, plant & machinery, methods, techniques, information, and a plan. Finally, it is bounded by time period: a day, a week, a month or a year.

Projects are managed by project managers; they are responsible to initiate, design, complete and manage them. They mobilize resources, decide timings of various activities and provide guidance to people working in the project.

Andersen and his colleagues (1995) argue that project management involves planning, organizing and controlling. Planning involves deciding in advance what to do when to do, where to do, and who is to do. Organizing encompass assigning the responsibilities of a project team to constituent members. And controlling the entire project i.e. ensuring that things are done according to plan, and taking corrective actions in case of any discrepancy.

Thus, there are three critical elements in project management: planning, organizing and controlling. Planning is the first step; hence, its effectiveness influences subsequent phases and ultimately performance of the project as well as organization.

Given that, it may be worthwhile to look into project planning so that the rate of success of a project can be increased. Therefore, this research is about project planning and its impact on project / organizational performance, at least theoretically because the research is using secondary data for analysis.

The rest of the document discusses previous research, research question, research objectives, research method, and importance of the research and outcome.

Research question

There are hundreds and thousands of problems and issues in the world; the human being is trying to resolve them with limited resources. In the same way, a piece of research is meant to address a problem and if possible suggest a plausible solution. Problems are expressed in a number of ways; a patient says "I have got headache", "I do not feel appetite", "I feel sick", etc. An economist may say a country is poor, underdeveloped, has lack of resources and son on.

Similarly, a researcher defines a problem in the form of a research question or statement because research question is "the first step (in the development of the proposal) is to define the issue or problem to be addressed in clear and precise terms so that there can be no ambiguity about what is to be attempted" (Baker, 2000). Cadman (2002) describes key characteristics of a research question, "concise, focused research question, the most important feature … as it acts as a road map for the rest of the Proposal". Ghauri et al state research question "indicates gaps in the scope or the certainty of our knowledge" (Ghauri, 1995).

Since the research is about project planning, the research problem can be stated in the following words,

What is project planning and how it affects performance of a project or organization?

Baker (2000) says that a number of key aspects/words should stem from a research question. The above research question has got two key words: project planning and its impacts on project / organizational performance. It suggests that the scope of the research will be limited to project planning literature and its impact on either project itself or on the entire organization. The secondary data will be applied for the purpose.

Research objectives

According to Corlien and others as summarized by Iqbal (2007) "research objective (s) provide focus, reduces the possibility to collect unnecessary data, organize the study in parts or phases" (Corlien et al, 2003), and develops a relationship between findings and practical applications (Online sources 2). The purpose of research question is to define the achievements of the research both to the discipline and the organisation/object being investigated.

Given that the objectives for this research are threefold:

- To investigate what is project management
- To explore what is project planning
- To identify what is the relationship between project planning and performance of the project or an organization

The first objective encompasses the broader area of research in order to provide a top-down understanding of the subject. The second objective indicates the focus of the research; purpose is to identify the importance of planning (methods and techniques) in project management. It is important to unveil the role of planning at this stage because it affects the subsequent steps in the process of project management. If this phase is strong than it would create positive effects on the remaining phases and vice versa. The third objective links project planning with performance of the project itself or the organization concerned. The performance determines the success or failure of a project. A recent survey shows that "agile software development projects have a 71.5% success rate, traditional projects a 62.8% success rate, and off shored software development projects a 42.7% success rate." (Ambler, 2008).

Research Method

Research method is the mean by which the solution of a research problem is sought. It is also a vehicle for achieving objectives of research, the success criteria of a research endeavour.

There are number of research methods available to a researcher: case study, survey and content analysis etc. A case study looks into a topic in detail in an organizational environment. It tries to create understanding of the phenomenon over a longer period of time. Case study also requires a suitable organization which may be studied to grasp the understanding. Interviews are the most common technique of data collection; documents and internal surveys can also be used to corroborate data. Interviews are transcribed, themes are identified and analysis is made by applying qualitative techniques. A survey is based upon a list of questionnaires that is distributed to relevant or prospective respondents. They fill it out and return to the researcher. Statistical instruments are used to analyze data. Content analysis is based upon published data or information about the subject. The researcher identifies relevant information and analyzes them in line with his / her topic. Both quantitative and qualitative techniques can be used for analysis.

Since the former two methods are used mostly in primary research, therefore, they are not suitable for this research. However, findings of past studies (case studies and surveys) will be used in the thesis to support the topic. A case study is not suitable for this work because it needs a longer period of time and is meant to look into the phenomenon in-depth.

The time period for this research is limited and does not allow researcher to conduct a detailed study on the topic. Survey is meant to do a piece of primary research that is not a requirement for this project. Conducting survey is costly and respondent return questionnaires after a while; a concern of time, because the researcher is not sure how long the respondents would take to return questionnaire. It suggests that both case study and survey are not

suitable for the researcher. Therefore, content analysis seems an appropriate option because secondary data are available and the researcher has access to its sources. The researcher believes that the project will be completed in-time.

Importance of the research and outcome

Iqbal (2007) suggests three areas as part of the importance of a research project:

- How it enhances the personal and professional development of the researcher?

- What is the theoretical contribution in the discipline concerned?

- What is the practical role in solving the problem?

A research project must contribute to the individual development of the researcher since he/she is the one who goes through the process of research i.e. selection of topic, data selection, data collection, data analysis, and presentation. The researcher also owns the piece of research. So the researcher would learn the process of research through this project. The second beneficiary of the research would be the discipline concerned. For instance, this research is about project management; the research would add something to the existing repository of the subject. Something means some sources will be collated together about project management that can be shared with the research community. It will be theoretical contribution to the discipline concerned. The third recipient of the research will be the university where the research is being submitted. Finally, the research is addressing a particular problem; the researcher would try to provide answer to it. Thus, a theoretical problem will be resolved.

REFERENCES

Alshawi, Mustafa and Bingunath Ingirige 2003. Web-enabled project management: an emerging paradigm in construction, Automation in Construction, 12, 349-364.

Ambler, Scott W. 2008. IT Project Success Rates Survey Results: August 2007, http://www.drdobbs.com.

Andersen, E S, Kristoffer V Grude and Tor Haug 1995. Goal Directed Project Management, Kogan Page, London.

Baker, M.J. 2000. Writing a Research Proposal, *The Marketing Review,* I (1), 61-75.

Cadman, K. 2002. English for Academic Possibilities: the research proposal as contested site in postgraduate genre pedagogy, *Journal of English for Academic Purposes*, 1(2), 85 –104.

Corlien, M. V. et al, 2003. Proposal Development and Fieldwork, Designing and conducting health systems research projects: volume 1, The International Development Research Centre (IDRC), Canada.

Evaristo, R. and P C van Fenema 1999. A typology of project management: emergence and evolution of new forms, International Journal of Project Management, 17(5), 275 – 28.

Ferns, D C 1991. Developments in programme management, *International Journal of Project Management,* (*9(3), 148-156.*

Ghauri, P. et al 1995. *Research methods in business studies,* London: Prentice Hall.

Hameri, Ari-Pekka 1997. Project management in a long-term and global one-of-a-kind project, International Journal of Project Management, 15(3), 151-157.

House, R S 1988. *The clean Side of Project Management,* Addison-Wesley, USA.

Iqbal J 2007. "Learning from a Doctoral Research Project: Structure and Content of a Research Proposal" *The Electronic Journal of Business Research Methods,* 5(1), 11 - 20, available online at www.ejbrm.com.

Johns, Thomas G 1995. Managing the behavior of people working in teams Applying the project-management method, International Journal of Project Management, 13(1), 33-38.

Juran, J M, 1989. Juran on Leadership for Quality: An Executive Handbook, Free Press, New York, NY.

White, D and J. Fortune 2002. Current Practices in Projects management – an empirical study, International Journal of Project Management, 20(5), 1 – 11.

Zwikael, O, Kazuo Shimizu and Shlomo Globerson 2005. Cultural differences in project management capabilities: A field study, International Journal of Project Management, 23(6), 454 – 462.

3 IMPACT OF INFORMATION TECHNOLOGY ON PROJECT MANAGEMENT (PM)[2]

Introduction

Information technology emerged as a vital organizational resource in the early 1980s (Friedman and Cornford, 1989). It became a source of competitive advantage in the business world (Porter & Miller, 1985). IT is a driving force redesigning and even redefining business solutions in contemporary organizations (Vanketraman, 1991). Technology is the fundamental enabler of social and economic change (Caron et al, 1994).

Project management is a unique endeavor designed to achieve a specific objective within given time and resources. It involves planning, organizing, and control of a venture (Andersen et al, 1995).

---

[2] Written for classroom discussion and dissemination to research students.

Azzopardi (2010) while discussing the historical development in project management states,

The 1980s and 1990's are characterized by the revolutionary development in the information management sector with the introduction of the personal computer (PC) and associated computer communications networking facilities. This development resulted in having low cost multitasking PCs that had high efficiency in managing and controlling complex project schedules. During this period low cost project management software for PCs became widely available that made project management techniques more easily accessible.

The Internet technology is supporting various stages of project management for coordination of project phases. Software packages help improves time and application of other resources. However, it requires a more detailed account of finding a relationship between IT and project management. Therefore, the objective of the research is to find out impacts of technology on project management practices.

The proposal discusses different components of a research: literature review, research question, research objectives, research method, and structure of the proposed dissertation.

Literature review

Project is the planning, organizing and controlling of project, a temporary endeavor to achieve organizational objective (Andersen et al, 1995; PMI, 2004). According to Hutson "modern project management is the third element of organizational management systems that is bringing balance, harmony, and success in global organizations" (Hutson, 1997). However, project management (PM) is not applicable in small project (WikiAnswers, 2010). It is largely perceived that PM is an advantageous discipline and business tool.

There are several inputs in the process of managing projects, for instance, human resources, plant and equipment, material and others (Hartman and Skulmoski, 1999). Technology is one of the recent additions to manage contemporary projects. For example, databases, CASE tools, project management software such as MS Project, inventory management and CAD for designing developmental projects, to name a few. The purpose of these technological instruments is to enhance the performance of projects since traditionally projects are notorious for budget overrun, consuming more time and not meeting quality standards. IT reduces the possibility of these issues. However, technology is a mixed blessing; it cost a lot, software support may not be timely which can delay a project (VIP Task manager, 2010). Thus, it loses the promise of cost effectiveness. Nevertheless, the negative impacts are diminishable.

Research question (RQ)

A piece of research always addresses a real world or hypothetical problem, which implies that the starting point of a research is the identification of such problem or question. Baker (2000) argues that a research question is "the first step (in the development of the proposal) is to define the issue or problem to be addressed in clear and precise terms so that there can be no ambiguity about what is to be attempted". It clarifies the issue to be resolved or at least an attempt to do so. There are certain characteristics of a research question;

according to Cadman (2002), it should be "concise, focused research question ... acts as a road map for the rest of the Proposal". It must "indicates gaps in the scope or the certainty of our knowledge" (Ghauri et al, 1995). The research question creates a relationship between research objectives and research method; a good research question specifies the method of data collection and consequently the data analysis mechanism. It also indicates the achievements of a piece of research in more specific terms. In this way, it defines the outcome or provides clues for a prospective outcome. Finally, RQ stems from the existing literature, its roots lie in the research already done to make it valuable in the research community.

Having been said this it can be argued that there were two parts of the research project i.e. IT and project management. The researcher tries to explore the relationship between them, which are expressed in the following words.

How information technology is applied in project management to improve its performance over its life cycle?

Some scholars argue that some key words should stem from a question; three key words are obvious in the above question: information technology, project management, and performance. There is a relationship between application of technology in projects management practices because it increases the performance of the project concerned. The research is an attempt to examine the relationship.

Research objectives

Research objectives define the possible or expected achievements of a research project. The purpose of research objective is to "provide focus, reduces the possibility to collect unnecessary data, organize the study in parts or phases" (Corlien et al, 2003). They create a relationship between research method and research question; which research method is appropriate for a particular objective. For example, a research objective expressed in quantitative terms requires use of a positivistic or objective method while description of objectives in a qualitative term requires interpretive methods of inquiry. They stem from the research question. The following objectives can be derived from our question and these objectives support the question.

- To find out what technological support is available to project managers.

- To find out how does IT enhance performance of project through application of technology?

- How the findings can be used to apply them in the similar settings in the future for higher performance?

The first objective demands a brief survey of the instrument of technology being used in project management theory as well as practices. For instance, software, the Internet, databases, and EDI etc. during various phases of project life cycle. The second objective is concerned with to know the application of technology in project planning, organizing, and control. The third objective provides the learning gained through the research exercise so that it may be used in the future in project management practices to improve the effectiveness of managing projects. As an example, Ambler (2008) believes that "agile software development projects have a 71.5%

success rate, traditional projects a 62.8% success rate, and off shored software development projects a 42.7% success rate".

Research method

Research method is the vehicle through which research question is resolved and the researcher achieves its objectives. There are a number of methods available for conducting a valid piece of research. Galliers (1992) classifies research methods, in connection with information systems/information technology perspective, into two categories: scientific and interpretive. He includes laboratory experiments, field experiments, surveys, case studies, theorem proof, forecasting and simulation in scientific paradigm while reviews, action research, descriptive/interpretive, future research and role/game playing under an interpretive group. Some of them look into a phenomenon in details such as case studies while others took a sample to analyse a topic i.e. surveys. The researcher plays a vital role in case studies since the interpretation depend upon the ability, experience and educational background of the researcher. While researchers design surveys who may be biased but the interpretation can be straightforward, therefore, remained unbiased.

Since the time and resources are limited for the research project, therefore, taking a detailed study is not possible, yet the researcher will conduct a mini case study in a retail setting. One of the retail stores will be examined for this purpose.

Rationale of the research and possible outcome

Technology has been a matter of concern in project management because most of the projects are launched for improving efficiency of an organization. However, the elements of the risk within a project jeopardize the expectations of success, therefore, it is necessary to reduce the probability of risk as much as possible. Technology can help to make it happen. The research would identify various technologies which can help managers to improve the performance of projects. Nevertheless, it is important to visualize the potential outcome of the research so that resources can be invested to achieve them.

In addition, Iqbal (2010) suggests three areas as part of the importance of a research project:

1. How it enhances the personal and professional development of the researcher?
2. What is the theoretical contribution in the discipline concerned?
3. What is the practical role in solving the problem?

A research project must contribute to the individual development of the researcher since he/she is the one who goes through the process of research i.e. selection of topic, data selection, data collection, data analysis, and presentation. The researcher also owns the piece of research. So the researcher would learn the process of research through this project. The second beneficiary of the research would be the discipline concerned. For instance, this research is about project management; the research would add something to the existing repository of the subject. Something means some sources will be collated together about project management that can be shared with the research community. It will be theoretical contribution to the discipline concerned. The third recipient of the research will be the university where the research is being submitted. Finally, the research is addressing a particular problem; the researcher would try to provide answer to it. Thus a theoretical problem will be resolved.

The researcher would try achieve these elements in addition to the objectives as defined in the above paragraphs.

Structure of the proposed dissertation

The thesis will be divided into six chapters:

The area of research (deals with research methodology, research problem and objectives)

Literature review (a brief survey of current work on the topic)

Introduction to project management

The role of IT in PM

Mini case study on application of IT in PM

Conclusion & recommendations

REFERENCES

Azzopardi, Sandro, 2010. *The Evolution of Project Management*. [online] Available at: http://www.buzzle.com/articles/evolution-project-management-business-organisations.html, [Accessed 12 October 2010].

Ambler, Scott W. 2008. *IT Project Success Rates Survey Results*. [online]Available at http://www.drdobbs.com. [Accessed 12 October 2010].

Andersen, E S, Kristoffer V Grude and Tor Haug 1995. *Goal Directed Project Management*, London: Kogan Page.

Baker, M.J. 2000. Writing a Research Proposal, *The Marketing Review,* I (1), 61-75.

Cadman, K. 2002. English for Academic Possibilities: the research proposal as contested site in postgraduate genre pedagogy, Journal of English for Academic Purposes, 1(2), 85–104.

Caron, J. R. et. al. 1994. Business Reengineering at CIGNA Corporation: Experience and Lesson Learned

From the First Five Years", *MIS Quarterly*, 18 (3), 233-50.

Corlien, M. V. et al, 2003. *Proposal Development and Fieldwork, Designing and conducting health systems research projects: volume 1*, The International Development Research Centre (IDRC), Canada.

Ghauri, P. et al 1995. *Research Methods in Business Studies*, London: Prentice Hall.

Galliers, R. D. 1992. *Choosing IS Research Approaches*, London: Blackwell Scientific Publications.

Greg, H. 2008. *Absolute Beginner's Guide to Project Management, Rough Cuts.* [online]QUE Publishing, Available at www.Quepublishing.com [Accessed 10 June 2010].

Greg, H. 2005. *Essential elements for managing any successful project*, [online]   QUE Publishing, Available at www.Quepublishing.com [Accessed 10 June 2010].

Friedman, A. L., and Cornford, D. S. 1989. *Computer Systems Development: History, Organisation, and Implementation*, New York: John Wiley & Sons.

Hutson, N. 1997. What is project management?, Project Management Institute, Upper Darby, PA.

Iqbal Javed, 2007. Learning from a Doctoral Research Project: Structure and Content of a Research Proposal, *The Electronic Journal of Business Research Methods*, 5 (1), 11 – 20.

Iqbal, Javed 2010. Managing Strategic Change: A real world case study, LAP Lambert Academic Publishing, Germany.

Meredith, J. and Mantel S J 2010. *Project Management: A Managerial Approach*, Singapore: John Wiley & Sons.

Porter, M E and V E Miller, 1985. How Information Gives you Competitive Advantage? *Harvard Business Review*, July-August.

Project management institute 2004. *A guide to the Project Management Body of Knowledge*, 3rd ed. Newton Square, PA: Project Management Institute.

Project management institute 2010. *Project institution documents*. [online] available at: www.mindtool.com [Accessed 21 June 2010].

Reiss, G. 1992. *Project Management Demystified*, London: Taylor & Francis.

UK Association of Project Management 1984. [online]   Available at: *www.apm.org.uk* [Accessed 12 October 2010].

Venkatraman, N. 1991. IT-induced Business Reconfiguration. In: Scott-Morton, M. S. *The Corporation of the 1990s, IT and Organization Transformation*, New York: Oxford University Press.

VikiAswers, 2010. *Advantages and disadvantages of project management?* [online] Available at: VikiAnswers.com [Accessed, 12 October 2010].

VIP Task Manager, 2010. Project *management software advantages and disadvantages*. [online] Available   at: http://www.taskmanagementsoft.com/solutions/project-management/project-management-software-advantages-and-disadvantages.php [Accessed 12 October 2010].

4 TECHNOLOGY DEVELOPMENTS IN SOUTH ASIA (SA): THE CASE OF PAKISTAN[3]

Introduction

The mission of the case is to explore the technological developments that took place in Pakistan in the South Asian perspective. The concern is to identify the impacts of these technologies on social, economic and political dimensions. And to find out the areas that need more attention to increase the pace of development and role of or potential contribution of technology in the process.

Technology played a pivotal role in the human development, especially in the last century. The new millennium revolutionized the process of technology-based innovations where technology

---

[3] Submitted for a chapter in a book

became a springboard for advancement of mankind on the planet and beyond. Notable advancements encapsulate medical science, information technology, food production, preservation and distribution (Hidellage, 2003). Technology explored the unknown frontiers in the four corners of the world that has been reduced to the extent where most of the dwellers of the earth can reach its boundaries with little efforts and investments.

However, the North harvested the maximum benefit of digital revolution; the South is still struggling to realize the true benefits of the change. Inhabitants of the South are looking towards the technology to address their chronic problems. The South Asia is the home of 22% of the world population but 44% of the poor; they wait for the miracles of technology to eliminate or minimize the dysfunctional impacts on their day-to-day lives (Gunasena, 2003). The key issues encompass elimination of poverty, shortage of energy, improvement of health services, reduction of illiteracy and availability of sufficient food for the masses. Off them, poverty has been on the top of the list (Paul, 2003) because it is a complex issue for both technology and politicians.

The focus of technology in the SA revolves around six areas: information technology, agriculture, building/construction, energy, transportation and water and waste (SARID, 2010). Each of these dimensions can be examined through three angles: invention, application, and diffusion.

The chapter deals with development of information technology in Pakistan. The purpose of investigation is to identify the developments that took place in the country over a period of last thirty years from 1980-2010 because the technology was diffused after the 1980s. It is followed by the examination of impacts on human life in the country. It may unveil the contribution of technology on social, political, and economic dimensions. Thus the chapter would concentrate on the areas where more investment/attention is needed to realize the potential of technology. It is in line with the Ministry of Science and Technology's project of Technology Foresight; the project is implemented through Pakistan Technology Board and the author was a member of the group established for the purpose.

One of our colleagues identified the role of technology in a number of sectors in Pakistan: good governance and strategic management, economic stability, high agricultural yield, industrial energy, poverty alleviation, and positive impact on international foreign policies (Qazi, 2004). Thus these factors are the subject of examining the impacts of technology. One example is being described in the following lines.

Technology becoming a backbone for good governance; National Database Registration Authority (NADRA) maintains the biometric records of about 90% of adult population of the country. In some areas like Azad Jammu and Kashmir the registration reached to 99%, it is followed by Punjab 91%, (APP, 2010). Computerized National Identity Cards (CINC) are used in many day-to-day activities of public such as buying a new mobile phone contract, driving license, voting, opening a bank account, admission in an educational institute like college, university, getting employed etc. It is argued that the initiative "would bring transparency in all social, political and economic affairs besides providing the vital health, education and social information for initiating targeted development programmes ... Banks in Pakistan are also flourishing because they know the identity of all their account holders, the official said and added crimes have been unearthed after tracing the identity of criminals' mobile phones that are issued after verification of their CNICs ... Meanwhile, the news site while quoting sources reported that there are around 90 data centralization projects in the queue at NADRA, which will ultimately enable all the data of several dozen departments linked with CNIC number" (APP, 2010). NADRA's next project is to link all the government departments together to facilitate all aspects of governance in the country, one official states that "in coming years this single identity will serve for tracking academic, health, driving license, family, insurance, internet, and so many other records." (ibid., p.1).

This is an example of the way technology is contributing for good governance. The paper or chapter would examine the other aspects of technology as well and how it affects the lives of people in the country. The tentative outlines of the chapter may contain the following elements: historical developments of different technologies (information technology, agriculture, building / construction, energy, transportation, water and waste), impacts of technology on social, economic and political dimensions of people: poverty alleviation, e-governance / good governance and international relations, for example. It will be followed by discussion and conclusion.

REFERENCES

Associate Press of Pakistan (APP) (2010) Around 90 % adult population registered with NADRA, http://www.app.com.pk/en_/index.php?option=com _content&task=view&id=108045&Itemid=2

Gunasena, H.P.M. (2003) FOOD AND POVERTY: TECHNOLOGIES FOR POVERTY ALLEVIATION, *South Asia Conference on Technologies for Poverty Reduction, New Delhi, 10 –11 October 2003.*

Hidellage, Vishaka (2003) IS THERE A NEED FOR A SOUTH ASIAN RESPONSE ON

TECHNOLOGY FOR POVERTY REDUCTION?, *South Asia Conference on Technologies for Poverty Reduction, New Delhi, 10 –11 October 2003.*

Paul, R (2003) SECTORAL TRENDS IN THE WATER SECTOR (TECHNOLOGY, POLICY, AND POVERTY) IN SOUTH ASIA, *South Asia Conference on Technologies for Poverty Reduction, New Delhi, 10 –11 October 2003.*

SARID, (2010) Appropriate Technology Sectors, South Asia Research Institute for Policy and

Development,
http://www.sarid.net/technology/appropriate/index.htm

Qazi, Wajahat Mahmood (2004) ROLE OF
INFORMATION TECHNOLOGY IN THE
DEVELOPMENT OF PAKISTAN,
http://www.khwarzimic.org/takveen/index.asp

5 MANAGEMENT INFORMATION SYSTEMS (SYNOPSIS)[4]

1. ABSTRACT

A book on the subject with Pakistani perspective is needed since teachers, students and professionals are using books written by foreign authors. They portray their local business and technical environment that is difficult to understand in the local academic and socio-economic perspective. The proposed book is an attempt to fill the gap because it provides local example on various topics. Thus the purpose of the books is to provide knowledge of the discipline within the local circumstances. In addition, foreign books are purchased through

---

[4] Submitted to a publisher for the publication of a book.

foreign exchange; the book will save precious hard currencies that may be spent on other necessary requirements.

Advanced nations of the world developed through self-sufficiency in every walk of life. The book may be able to lead towards self-sufficiency in the discipline. The project will also trigger other experts of the discipline/subject to write more comprehensive books on the subject. It also becomes a driver for researches to conduct research in the industry on the related topics discussed in the book.

1-FEATURE OF THE BOOK

The length of the book is about 300-350 pages divided into ten chapters. Each chapter has 6000-8000 words or 25-30 pages (A-4).

Each chapter begins with learning objectives in order to comprehend what is required of this chapter. Introduction provides brief introduction of the contents of the chapter.

The body of each chapter has been arranged logically so that various topics should flow in a natural and easy to understandable manner. Short sentence has been constructed to avoid complexity of language. Williams and Sawyer (2005) say they have limited their sentences in their book to 20-22 words. The same principle has been applied in the book.

Plenty of diagrams and tables have been used to grab key point in a summarized version. Every topic has been illustrated with a pictured diagram since "one picture is better than one thousand words". Diagrams have been drawn to illustrate key concepts, theories, models and frameworks. Appropriate colors scheme has been applied to grab the attention of the readers.

Each chapter is concluded with "implications for managers". The purpose is to shed light on the topic from managerial point of view or how concepts and theories discussed in the chapters are applicable in industry, and how managers can apply them.

It is followed by a summary, a brief introduction of the material discussed in the chapter.

The case study is a popular instrument for teaching and understanding text material. All the cases have been taken from the local business and economic environment. Therefore, the learning material has been augmented with a case study, a local scenario of the particular topic. Also, some short case studies have been included in the body of the text in the form of "boxes"

Each chapter starts with a framework for describing and analysis of concepts included in the chapters.

Each chapter provides review and discussion questions in order to encourage class discussion and review for examination.

Each chapter provides list of sources consulted to compile that chapter. The reader can enhance their knowledge of the chapter through consulting references provided. Original intention was to keep the number of references to thirty for each chapter, however, some chapters went beyond the limit and some remained under the limit. The total number is more than 300.

2. SCOPE

A survey of five books taught in Pakistani higher education institutes on the subjects was the basis of forming the syllabus. Apart from the introductory chapter (chapter1), other chapters are the common topics being taught in the country in one semester. In addition, teaching of the subject over last many years provides insight that which core topics must be included in an MIS book have been included in this text. From practitioners' point of view, a manager should know something about the field so that he can understand reports prepared for him. For example, kinds of information systems have been discussed in chapter four. A manager must know how various types of information can be collected, analyzed and conveyed to him. By knowing that he can ask for the shape/form of information he desired to see/read. To illustrate further, a senior manager is interested in internal and external information about his organization, his industry, the entire economy, and the world economy so that he can form an opinion about the performance of his organization. For example, if industry returns on investment (ROI) is 8% and his company is earning 9% then he will be comfortable about his company's performance. On the contrary, if his organization is making 6% ROI he must be concerned about it and should take appropriate measures to enhance it.

Some endeavours are measured through qualitative measures; some are undertaken in response a competitive threat.

3. LITERATURE REVIEW

Since there is no book available on the topic in Pakistan which can be included in the literature review, however, some research has been done on the individual topics included in the proposed book.

Some articles are written on e-commerce; the Business Recorder, a daily newspaper had published a supplement on e-commerce. The author had consulted it and included some material of it. In telecommunication industry website of Pakistan Telecommunication Authority (PTA) is quite helpful because it provides up to date data about telecom-industry and related matters.

4-CONTENTS

1. Relevance with HEC Approved Curriculum

It is one of the core subjects being taught in universities and higher education institutes. Therefore, it lies under the HEC approved scheme.

2. Table of contents

Please see attachment, TABLE OF CONTENTS.

3. Two draft sample chapters

Please see attachment, TWO DRAFT CHAPTERS.

4. Research methodology (especially for Monographs)

Not applicable because it is a text book.

5. CONTENDING BOOK TITLES

(a) Laudon K C and Laudon J P 2007. Management Information Systems, New Jersey: Pearson Education.

(b) O'brien, J A. 2007. Management Information Systems, Boston: McGraw-Hill Irwin.

(c) Oz, Effy 2007. Management Information Systems, Boston: Course Technology.

(d) Mcleod, R, and Jr. G.P. Schell 2007. Management Information Systems, Dehli: Pearson Education.

Table 1 Comparative analysis						
Book title	Author name	Publisher	Publication date	Price	Level	Category
Management Information Systems	Laudon K C and Laudon J P	Pearson Education	2007	PKR698	Graduate	Text book
Management Information Systems	O'Brien, J A	Course Technology	2007	PKR698	Graduate	Text book

Management Information Systems	Oz, Effy	Thomson	2007	PKR699	Graduate	Text book
Management Information Systems	McLeod, R and Jr. G.P. Schell	Pearson Education	2007	PKR330	Graduate	Text book

The proposed book will be different in that it provides local examples, case studies, and application to Pakistani managers about technical and social environment. Most of the competing titles describe more material than the amount taught in the local universities which make these titles bulky and ultimately expensive. All of them are written by American authors who are talking about a developed nation and quoting examples of an advanced country both economically and academically. Material presented at the end of each chapter i.e. review questions, case studies etc. have been written with the assumption that this will be absorbed by the local students, whereas local students are unable to absorb high quality examples, questions, and case studies. Also, English language is an issue for the local students since competing titles are written by native English speakers. Since English is the second language of the authors, he has constructed sentences accordingly and uses average level vocabulary which is easily understandable by the local readers. Students often complaint about the level of English used in the foreign books.

The amount of material, language, and easily comprehendible ending material are the strength of the text. The length of the text may be a weakness because competing titles cover more material than this work.

The material covered in the competing books is difficult to be taught in a single semester because it is beyond the capacity of the local student/readers. For example, most of this text contains 15 or 16 chapters which are a normal or a common practice in the USA that professors cover one chapter each week which their students can absorb. A semester consists of 15/16 weeks of 3 teaching hours each week. It makes or weight 3 credit hours which is a unit of measurement of academic achievement/input. Most of the teachers in Pakistan cover 9/10 topics or chapters, therefore, the syllabus has been kept as such, ten chapters.

Since there is no book available in the market written by a Pakistani author, thus there is an open gap both in academic and research field. If it is available (but it is not in my knowledge), even then the proposed work is a well-researched work which contains about three hundred references. Students and researcher would find it a reliable source of further work. The number of references is almost equivalent to a doctoral thesis. In addition, the proposed work offers up to date material since most of the reference material has been selected from after the turn of the century. The last century's material has been included in case no work was found after the current millennium.

It implies that the proposed work not only fills the academic and research gap in Pakistan but also adds value to the existing literature at international level. It is because the work is focusing on a given geographical area where little attention was given about the subject.

6-TARGET READERSHIP/ MARKET OF THE STUDY

The target of the book is both academia and practitioners. The contents have been selected carefully to include the common topics found in international books on the subject and taught in Pakistan for one semester duration.

The primary target of the work is undergraduate students of universities and degree awarding institutes. It implies that the professors are also a part of them since they will recommend and use it as a text book.

The secondary target of the book is managers at various levels in private and public sector. The section "implication for managers" has been included in the text for them exclusively.

The purpose of this section is to identify how managers can use the material covered in a particular chapter. Also, the framework included in the beginning of each chapter invites readers and managers how they can resolve their organizational problems with the help of the material discussed in the chapter. For instance, "management" in the framework implies: what are the managerial issues involved regarding this chapter. "Information" meant, what information is required to address these issue. And "systems" refer to the fact that how information systems help to utilize information to resolve these issues. In the next step "analysis" all these elements are put together to arrive at a feasible solution of the managerial issues discussed/referred to earlier.

The third target is present and potential researchers. The researchers can consult referred work provided at the end of each chapter or together at the end. As each chapter is a topic itself and has been equipped with thirty references, the researchers can identify and enhance their understanding of the material and may do further research on the topic.

7-OTHER REQUIREMENTS

a-Literature /Bibliography

Please see attachment, BIBLIOGRAPHY.

b-Bio Data Form of the Author and Co-Author (if any), also attached detailed Curriculum Vitae.

Please see attachment, BIO DATA FORM & CV.

c-A paragraph on the kind or type of subject specialist, who can best evaluate the monograph/textbook. (Do not suggest the name of evaluator)

The book is targeted at management sciences students, teachers, and managers. Therefore, the most suitable person would be one who is teaching the subject. He has the knowledge of the subject /contents and able to compare this work with the competing titles. Secondly, a manager or IT related manager can look at the material and evaluate it since one target of the book is practitioners as well.

Any suggestions from this evaluator would be a source of learning and improvement for the author.

d-Writers Conditions: Any proposal or condition/s the author/s may like to add.

e-Three (03) copies of book proposal (03 hard copies and soft copies, 01 CD).

f-A list of all enclosures:

a. Synopsis (this document)

b. Table of contents

c. Two draft chapter (chapter 1 and chapter 5)

d. Bibliography (chapter wise)

e. Chapter wise summary of all chapters

f. Bio data form and CV

g. CD

6 THE NATURE OF FAMILY BUSINESS IN PAKISTAN AND HOW IT CONTRIBUTES TOWARDS THE ECONOMIC (AND SOCIAL) DEVELOPMENT OF THE COUNTRY[5]

Abstract

The concept paper examines the long due need of industry-academia collaboration which is a necessity in developed countries because it improves the understanding between the pair to design educational programmes in line with the industry requirements. Purpose is to enhance productivity, a much needed commodity in the ear of global competition and ever increasing needs of the country. The objective of the research is to conduct case studies focusing on family owned businesses. The tacit knowledge residing in the minds of industry professionals need transformation to explicit knowledge so that masses may take benefit out of it. It will be accomplished through detailed

---

[5] Submitted to SMEDA for an industry-academia collaboration project.

analysis of the phenomenon to make it usable for existing and potential entrepreneurs and researchers. The data will be collected from the family-firm owners and professional managers through structured interviews. It will be corroborated through documents and possibly observations. Initially, the BELPAK located in Sialkot and is in the second generation of existence has been selected as a research setting for the project. The outcome will either be a research paper (s) or report. It will be available to the stakeholders and other interested individuals and organisations.

INTRODUCTION

Family business is the "traditional way of conducting business within the private sector" (Maudle 2008). FB is the "one where a family owns enough of the equity to be able to exert control over strategy and involved in the top management position". (Colli and Rose,) "An organization in which a family controls ownership and management and intends to pass these elements to the next generation." (Astrachan and Shanker, 2003)." The kind of small business started by one or few individuals who had an idea, worked hard to develop it, and achieved, usually with limited capital, growth while maintaining majority of the ownership of the enter prize (Babicky, 1987). "Any business in which decisions regarding its ownership or management are influenced by a relationship to a family or families." (Hollan and Oliver, 1992). Incorporated family firms are those where more than 50% of the share is owned by the family, two or more shareholders have the same surnames, and, at least one family shareholder is also a director; it also include "where the family directors make up more than 30% of the board (family-firm > 30%) and, secondly, where the family directors make up more than 50% of the board (family- firm > 50%) (Wilson et al, 2013). It suggests that family business is characterized with ownership, control, and succession. It is augmented with the commencement of a business or purchase of a certain business by the member of a family but expanded over time by increase in ownership or control.

Study of family business (FB) is important due to their contribution to the economic activity in Europe and elsewhere, greater awareness of the issue increased intricacies of business transfer and academic interest in the field. FB performs better than the corporate rivals (Ward, 1983) they have competitive advantage (Anderson and Reeb, 2003). Family firms compete and behave differently from those who are classed as non-family firms (Ward, 2004). Family businesses are "significantly less likely to fail than non-family firms." (Wilson et al, 2013)

It is equally important in Pakistan where most of the businesses are managed in private sector and virtually they are family owned. Pakistan is among ten top countries in the production of wheat, rice, cotton, and sugarcane; they are in the private ownership. A large number of them are owned by big families. Similarly, manufacturing, trade, and services are owned and managed by private or family owners. They are classified rich families; at times they were only a score but gradually increased over time. It is reported that 35 more milliners joined the club of International wealthier people in one year only. However, little attention has been paid neither on corporate sector nor on family business from the academia. Therefore, the purpose of the paper is to look into the matter as an attempt, to begin with, so that later researchers may inspire of it and it may trigger them to divert their attention towards this important but neglected field. It will be accomplished by a series of case studies in mutual consensus with SMEDA. The purpose of the study is to explore the phenomenon in a detailed manner; it includes the nature of family business in the local context and focus on the following research question.

What is the nature of family business in Pakistan and how it contributes towards the economic (and social) development of the country? And how can it be applied in similar or different situations to encourage future startups? The researcher wanted to know the makeup of the family business including business transfer and succession issues. Aim is to identify the contribution of FB in the economic development and its social impacts.

The SMEDA is interested in to examine the golden triangle i.e. Sialkot, Gujranwala, and Gujrat. It is because 60% of country's SMEs are located in the area. The initial search shows that BELPAK is a family owned business started in 1985 and is in the second generation. However, it is not known whether the pair of generations is managing it simultaneously or otherwise.

Objectives

Since the nature of the study is to explore the topic which seems qualitative in principle. Common purpose of such studies is to understand the phenomenon, therefore, the study focuses on the following objectives.

To understand the family business in general and in the local context

To identify the success factors and reasons of failure associated with the FB

To know how the findings may be applied to the existing FB and the possible future endeavors

The above achievements are the starting point; more robust outcome will be expected on the way to networking that would take place as a part of the research process.

Research method

Since the topic is qualitative in nature, therefore, a similar method seems appropriate. Case study is referred to as one of the famous qualitative approach to examine a business case in order to develop a plausible story. Yin (2013), a well-known figure on the subject believes that it is helpful when the issue or purpose is not very much clear or sometimes not known. Case study is a thick description of the phenomena in order to understand it within its context.

Data will be collected through documents and interviews. The primary source is interviews; at least interviewee from one family members of the firm under consideration. Twenty-five interviews will be conducted from the senior and middle managers outside the family circles. More family interviews will be desirable but it depends upon the availability of the family members who are busy people which makes it normally difficult. Data analysis would commence with transcription of interviews, identification of themes and making relationship between unconnected threads. Appropriate software will also be taken on board for analysis.

Outcome

The outcome of the research will be either a report summarizing the meaning, process, and findings of a given family business or a research paper. The findings will be the story of success of the family and the factors that contribute in the process.

The findings will be useful for the organization concerned in that they can fine tune their business strategy or learning process. Other organization can apply the outcome to harness their business strategies for binding and bridging their social capital. New entrepreneurs can use them to start their entrepreneurial activities. Other researchers can undertake similar work or further the same. They can explore undiscovered areas and can bring more empirical audience to the world. So a useful debate can take place.

Cost Analysis:

The cost is associated with data collection, analysis, and documentation. It depends upon the selection of firm i.e. if they are in Rawalpindi and Islamabad than travelling cost may be less than when it may be out of the city.

The cost consists of the following items:

- Travelling and Boarding of interviewer

- Remunerations to the researchers

The hardware and printing/binding facilities are available in the university; therefore, no cost is expected. Around Rs.31000 may be required to complete the research. It is expected that 25 interviews will be taken in about 9 days (3 interviews per day); the researcher is to stay 9 nights in the hotel which will cost Rs. 2000 per night. The researcher will be paid 1000 daily allowance. The one off travelling cost will be 3000.

REFERENCES

ColliI, A. Mary Rose (2007). Family Business, ch. 9 of the Oxford Handbook of Business History, G. Jones and J. Zeitlin (eds.), Oxford University Press, 2007.

Mandl, Irene (2008). Overview of Family Business Relevant Issues – Final Report, Austrian Institute for SME Research, European Commission, Enterprise and Industry Directorate-General.

Holland PG, Oliver JE (1992). An empirical examination of stages of development of family business. J Bus Entrepreneurship 4(3):27–38.

Shanker MC, Astrachan JH (1996). Myths and realities: Family businesses. Contribution to US economy. A framework for assessing family business statistics. Fam Bus Rev 9(2):107–123.

Skyscrapercity. Retrieved from: http://www.skyscrapercity.com/showthread.php?t=626393

Ward, J (2005). Unconventional Wisdom, Counterintuitive Insights for Family Business Success, London: John Wily and Sons Ltd.

Yin, R. (2013). Case Study Research: Design and Methods (Applied Social Research Methods), SAGE Publications, Inc; Fifth Edition edition.

Theworldtopten. Retrieved from: http://www.theworldtoptens.com/top-10-richest-people-of-pakistan-2013/

BELPAK, a customer focused company is engaged in the production of a wide range of Motorsports Apparel / Motorcycle Clothing, Gloves and related accessories.

Established in 1985 and founded by the C.E.O. Mr. Sheikh Saleem, the family owned company is now run by its second generation and headed by the young executive Mr. Sheikh Umer.

Although the setup of the company was quite small initially, the founders of the company had strong vision and urge to turn this small setup, into one of the renowned companies in the Motosports apparel manufacturing. Continuing to materialize its dream with strong managerial capabilities and dedicated workforce, BELPAK has achieved remarkable progress in the market and celebrating its 28th anniversary now.

Having a current workforce of 125 workers, complete in-house stitching machines setup, pattern making, R&D department and latest manufacturing technology, the quality of products is well versed with international standards and meet the CE protective criteria for the biker community.

The company is in its highly progressive phase and further expanding its infrastructure and workforce, in order to ensure it meets the increasing demand of its existing and potential new customers.

Keeping Social Responsibility at priority and Health & Safety in focus, BELPAK provides basic orientation to all its workers such as Neat & Clean working environment, Adequate Health Facilities, Regular worker vaccinations, Noise protection Equipment, Fire drills, and Emergency Exit trainings.

Believing in commitment towards quality and dedicated customer service, BELPAK welcomes you to the family of our satisfied valued partners, with best of cooperation and professional support from our entire Tea

7-ECONOMIC IMPACTS OF MOBILE PHONES IN SEVEN SOUTH ASIAN COUNTRIES: AN EXAMINATION OF THE PHENOMENON FROM 2004 TO 2013[6]

Abstract

The purpose of the research is to examine the impacts of mobile phones in several South Asian countries who are the members of South Asian Association for Regional Cooperation (SAARC). Ten years' time frame has been adopted because most of the development in the phenomenon was experienced during it. The secondary data from various sources such as ITU, World Economic Forum, sources from individual countries will be used to make analysis. The framework proposed by Donner (2008) is the basis for the research because it is simple and appropriate to the resource and time

---

[6] Submitted for post-doc research

constraints. It is expected that the research would contribute towards theoretical developments in the form of a model based upon the experience. It would also enhance the research capability of the researcher and will be helpful for career/advancement prospects. The study would improve the image of the University of Manchester through producing more value added work to its rich portfolio. The key contribution of the research is the examination of Foreign Direct Investment (FDI) and revenue from mobile telephony; both are contributing towards GDP, a measure of wellness of people of a country.

Keyword: Mobile phones, FDI, GDP, economic development, South Asia

Introduction

The most important technological development trend in the last decade has been the explosive growth of mobile phones (Duncombe, 2012). In economic terms, every 10% increase in mobile density enhances 0.60% increase in GDP in developing countries and 1% in developed nations (Aker and Mbiti, 2010). It enabled the poorest countries to extend their telecommunication network coverage to mass of their population (Duncobme, 2012). Mobile telephony saves expensive infrastructure that can be used elsewhere in developing countries (Drori, 2010). It is believed that there are 3.6 billion mobile users in 2009 (The Economist, 2009) which increase to 4.61 billion in 2016 (Statista.com, 2016).

Since the boom in the phenomenon has been experienced in developing countries more rapidly than the developed segment (The Economist, 2009), therefore, the focus of most of research endeavours was about the former. Aker and Mbiti (2010) worked on many African countries; De Silva and his colleagues (2008) on five Asian countries; Kathuria et al (2009) on India; Gao and Rafiq (2009) on Pakistan; Bairagi et al (2011) on Bangladesh. However, little efforts have been made to work on a group of countries in South Asia which is important for many reasons. First, the previous work about a group of countries was greatly acknowledged and in fact widely referred such as the work of Aker and Mbiti (2010); De Silva et al

(2008) etc. Second, the South Asia (Afghanistan, Bangladesh, India, Nepal, Myanmar, Pakistan and Sri Lanka) is the home of more than 2 billion inhabitants. India and Pakistan are the emerging economies (The economist, 2014). The fastest growth in mobile phone has been recorded in Pakistan in the world (Haq, 2010). So it is worthwhile to examine the development of the mobile technology in order to fill the research gap that exists in the area because the empirical evidence of the relationship between the proposed variables is limited in literature. Therefore, the purpose of the research is to understand the phenomenon from a wider perspective for policy implications. Thus, the outcome will be useful for researchers, policy articulators, and decision makers in the industry and at the country level. It may also trigger foreign direct investment (FDI) from the international agencies and organizations through knowing pros and cons of the telecom sector.

The proposal has been structured as follows: the following section seeks the theoretical support for the work; the third section discusses the methodological debate. The final provides the sources of survey of literature.

Literature review

Mobile phone is a short wave telecommunication consists of a subscriber and the service provider as a wireless connection through a transmitter (Cooper, 1973). It is a combination of many channels such as voice call, text message, and email. In other words, it uses sound, images, and symbols to enable one or more individuals/teams to exchange them (Chattratichart and Brodie, 2003). Mobile telephone technology offers less developed countries an opportunity to install relatively cheap telecommunication infrastructure which saves scare resources that can be utilized in more hungry areas (Druri, 2010). Mobile phones trigger employment, promotion of social cohesiveness, empowerment, improving education/literacy, coping with natural disasters and promoting social responsibility (Bairagi, Roy and Polin, 2011). Mobile phones outnumbered the land line in 2002 (Donner, 2008). ITU (2003) emphasizes its importance in the following word,

the greatest impact of mobile communications on access to communication services—in other words, increasing the number of people who are in reach of a telephone connection of any kind—can be seen in developing countries ... In countries where mobile communications constitute the primary form of access, increased exchange of information on trade or health services is contributing to development goals; in countries where people commonly use both fixed-line and mobile communications, the personalized traits of the mobile phone are changing social interaction.

The phenomenon has been studied from economic and social dimensions. From economic perspective one of them is known as "impact assessment" (IA). It has been defined by Kirkpatrick & Hulme (2001) as "the process of identifying the anticipated or actual impacts of a development intervention, on those social, economic and environmental factors which the intervention is designed to affect or may inadvertently affect". Duncombe (2009) related with the work of Hulme (2000) and put forward a framework for analysis of impact which consists of three variables: readiness, availability and uptake, and impact. However, they are too complex to operationalize and implement. The framework needs cost/benefit analysis to determine the value of outcome.

Donner (2008) has examined mobile phenomenon from three dimensions: mobile phone adoption (as a dependent variable), mobile phone's impact (mobile phones as independent variables) and mobile phone interrelationships (emerged or ensemble approaches). They have been studied from two aspects. The first is known as Information and Communication Technology for Development (ICT4D); it focuses on digital divide, universal access, economic growth, livelihood, and evaluation or design of ICTD projects. The second has been classified as non-ICTD strategy; it deals with liberalization of mobile sector, diffusion/adoption, education, emergencies, medicine, appropriation, everyday life, globalization and design in context. Economic growth falls under the former (i.e. ICT4D) strategy and is related with impacts of mobile. The aim of studies about growth is to examine "the ways in which mobile use accelerates, complicates, or otherwise interacts with the process of economic development". (Donner, 2008) For instance, Waverman, Meschi, and Fuss (2005) examined the relationship between mobile phone penetration and its impacts on GDP. Another team of researchers examined the effects of mobile phones on production efficiency in developing countries

(Thompson and Garbacz, 2007). William (2005) investigated the penetration of mobile phones and flow of foreign direct investment (FDI). These studies can be ranked under the umbrella of macro-economic level (Aker and Mbiti, 2010).

This study aims at to focus on the economic growth from the work of Donner (2008) i.e. mobile as independent variable in macro-economic perspectives. It is required because there are few such analyses available in the region so far. Iqbal (2011) examined it from a broader point of view rather than focusing on mobile phones. In addition, it may also inspire other researchers to take the work further. The model for the has been discussed in the following section.

Research design / framework

This section includes basic premises such as research question, objectives, data collection and analysis strategy. And a theoretical framework to achieve research objectives and answer the research question in an appropriate manner.

The research would address the following research question:

What are the economic impacts of mobile phones in seven South Asian countries from 2004 to 2013?

The objective is to understand the issue by concentrating on some specific goals such as:

To identify the penetration of mobile phones in the region over a given period of time i.e. from 2004 to 2013.

To identify economic impacts of the technology on the respective countries.

To identify the barriers for adoption/diffusion of mobile phones and to recommend a way forward.

To suggest a model for the expansion of the technology in the countries concerned based upon the experience of the research.

The data will be collected from the secondary sources: ITU, world economic forum, the Internet stat, the World Bank, and CIA world fact book. The country data will be collected and may be corroborated from the internal sources such as the Statistical Bureaus, Central Banks, Telecom authorities, mobile phone companies, ISPs etc. The previous research will be a source as well.

Analysis will be based upon the guidelines of Miles and Huberman (1994), Sauro (2012) and Frost (2013). The first level of analysis will include horizontal analysis and vertical analysis in the form of comparisons, percentages, and averages. The statistical analysis revolves around SPSS v 22; the focus will be on factor analysis, correlation/ regression and possibly co-linearity. Alpha values would provide the internal validity while the external validity will be solicited from the previous research.

The study is based upon four variables: mobile density (penetration), FDI, mobile revenue and GDP. The last one will be the dependent variables while others play the role of predictors (independent variables). Figure 1 below depicts a pictorial relationship of these variables.

All the variables are grounded in the literature. Number 1 above has been identified by Donner (2008), Waverman, Meschi, and Fuss (2005) worked on the relationship i.e. Number 3 and William (2005) researched relation of FDI and mobile phones, Number 2. Other studies are also supporting the constituents of the model. Kathuria, et al (2009) applied similar parameters for economic analysis of mobile's impact in India. Their fundamental premises of analysis are the mobile penetration and development overtime while the dependent variable is GDP and state levels. However, they did not include FDI which also creates indirect impacts on GDP through capital and job generation; both contribute to GDP. Aker and Mbiti (2010) also used "mobile phone coverage and adoption" for the analysis of economic impacts of mobile phones in Africa.

The scope of the study is limited to the courtiers and the time frame within the impacts of mobile. It is a quantitative (positivistic) study in principle, however; some aspects will be interpreted qualitatively if it is required.

REFERENCES

Aker, Jenny C. and Isaac M. Mbiti (2010). Mobile Phones and Economic Development in Africa, Journal of Economic Perspectives, 24(3),207-32.

Bairagi, Anupam Kumar, Tuhin Roy *and* Afroza Polin (2011). Socio-Economic Impacts of Mobile Phone in Rural Bangladesh: A case Study in Batiaghata Thana, Khulna District, IJCIT, 2(1), 42-48.

Chattratichart, Jarinee. & Brodie, Jacqueline. (2003). *Envisioning a Mobile Phone for 'All' Ages.* Published by IOS Press, (c) IFIP, 725-728.

Cooper, M. (1973). *Cellular Phone.* General Manager of Motorola's Communications system.http://searchmobilecomputing.techtarget.c om/sDefinition/0,,sid40_gci211763,00.html ion

Donner, Jonathan (2008). Research Approaches to Mobile Use in the Developing World: A Review of the Literature, The Information Society, 24(3), 140-159.

Drori, G.S. (2010). Globalization and Technology Divides Bifurcation of Policy between the "Digital

Divide" and the "Innovation Divide". *Sociological Inquiry*, 80(1), 63–91.

Duncombe, R (2012). Understanding Mobile Phone Impact on Livelihoods in Developing Countries: A New Research Framework, Centre for Development Informatics, Institute for Development Policy and Management, SED, University of Manchester, Arthur Lewis Building, Manchester, M13 9PL, UK.

De Silva, H., Zainudeen, A. & Ratnadiwakara D. (2008). Perceived economic benefits of telecom access at the Bottom of the Pyramid in emerging Asia, LIRNEasia (www.lirneasia.net).

Frost, Jim (2013). Regression Analysis: How Do I Interpret R-squared and Assess the Goodness-of-Fit?, [Online] Available: http://blog.minitab.com/blog/adventures-in-statistics/regression-analysis-how-do-i-interpret-r-squared-and-assess-the-goodness-of-fit (December 25, 2013)

Gao P & Adnan Rafiq (2009). Analysing the Mobile Telecommunications Market in a Developing Country: *A Socio-Technical Perspective on Pakistan*, Centre for Development Informatics, Institute for Development Policy and Management, SED,

University of Manchester, Arthur Lewis Building, Manchester, M13 9PL, UK.

Haq, R (2010) Cell Phones Boost Pakistan's Literacy, Economy, [Online] Available: http://www.riazhaq.com.

Kathuria, R et al (2009). An econometric analysis of the impact of mobile, In Vodafobe (2009) India: The Impact of Mobile Phones, The Policy Paper Series Number 9, Published by Vodafone Group Plc, ISBN 978-0-9552578-5-8.

Hulme, D (2000). Impact Assessment Methodologies for Microfinance: Theory, Experience and Better Practice, World Development, 28(1), 79-98.

Iqbal, Javed (2011). *Digital Divide in South Asia*, Manchester: GRaASS Books.

Iqbal, Javed (2013). Information and Communication Technology: A Comparison of Pakistan and Sri-Lanka, Œconomica, 9(2), 9-22.

Kirkpatrick, C. & Hulme, D. (2001). *Basic Impact Assessment at Project Level*, Enterprise Development Impact Assessment Information Service, University of Manchester. [Online]

Available:
www.sed.manchester.ac.uk/research/iarc/ediais/word-files/LETSReferences.doc   Accessed 12/02/2009.

Miles, M B. & Huberman, A M. (1994). Qualitative Data Analysis (2nd edition). Thousand Oaks, CA: Sage Publications.

Sauro, Jeff (2011). How to interpret survey responses: 5 techniques, [Online] Available: http://www.measuringusability.com/blog/interpret-responses.php (December 2, 2013).

Sridhar, Kala Seetharam, and Varadharajan Sridhar (2006). Telecommunications and growth: Causal model, quantitative and qualitative evidence. *Economic and political weekly:* 2611-2619.

Statista 2016. [Online] Available:
http://www.statista.com/statistics/274774/forecast-of-mobile-phone-users-worldwide/

The Economist (2014). The Markets & Data, [Online] Available: http://www.economist.com/markets-data.

The Economist (2009). Mobile marvels,   [Online] Available:

http://www.economist.com/node/14483896

Thompson, Herbert, and Christopher Garbacz (2007). Mobile, fixed line and internet service effects on lobal productive efficiency. *Information Economics and Policy* 19 (2), 189-214.

Vodafobe (2009). India: The Impact of Mobile Phones, The Policy Paper Series Number 9, Published by Vodafone Group Plc, ISBN 978-0-9552578-5-8.

Waverman, Leonard, Meloria Meschi, and Melvyn Fuss. (2007). *The impact of telecoms on economic growth in developing nations.* Moving the Debate Forward: The Vodafone Policy Paper Series #3 2005 [Online] Available:

http://www.vodafone.com/etc/medialib/attachments/cr_downloads.Par.78351.File.tmp/GPP_SIM_paper_3.pdf.

Williams, M (2005). Mobile networks and Foreign Direct Investment in developing countries, In Africa: The Impact of Mobile Phones, The Policy

Paper Series Number 3, Published by Vodafone Group Plc.

APPENDIX IMAGES OF WEBSITES REFERING THE ARTICLE

1-The Deakin University Australia. It ranked the article as an excellent piece of work on the subject (Exhibit A1 and A2).

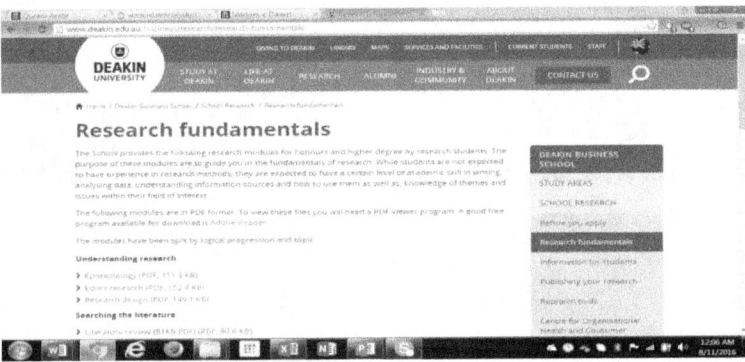

Exhibit A1

Exhibit A2

2-DeVilgo University in the sources of information (Exhibit A3)

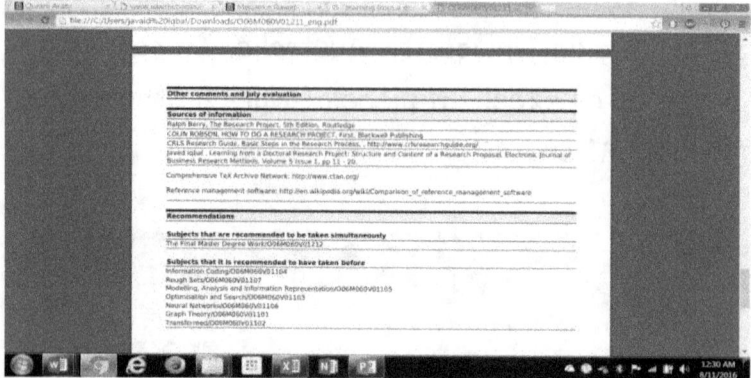

Exhibit A3

3-Report of five Universities of Lithuania (Exhibit A4)

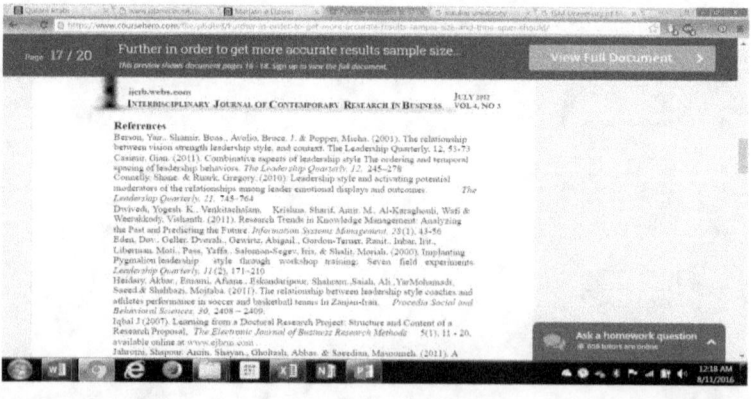

Exhibit A4

4-Lovely University in its recommended list of compulsory reading (Exhibit A5)

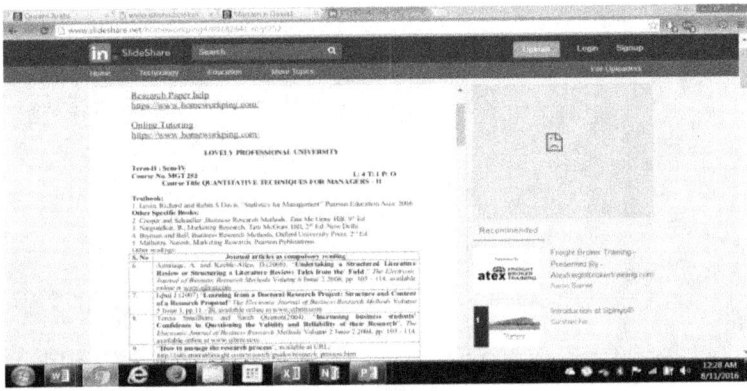

Exhibit A5

5-Singapore Management University in its list of sources for dissertation/thesis research and writing articles (Exhibit A6)

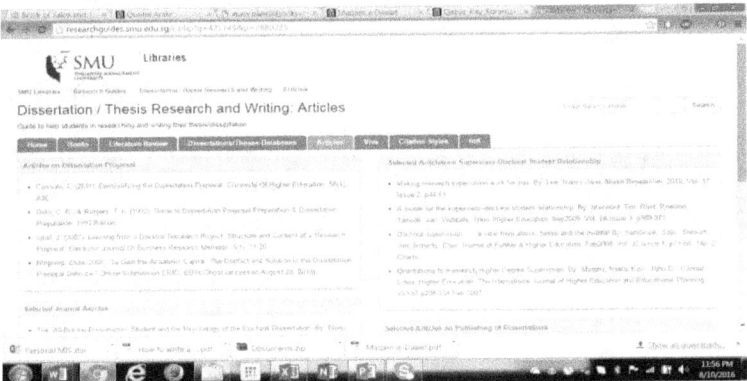

Exhibit A6

6-Proceeding of a Sri Lankan University (Exhibit A7)

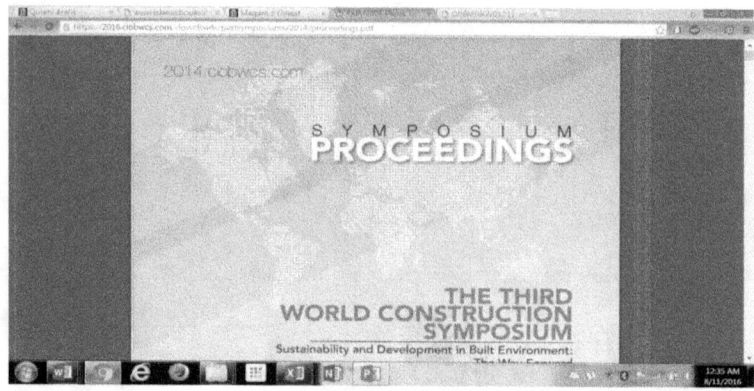

Exhibit A7

7-Adminstrative Issues Journal (Exhibit A8)

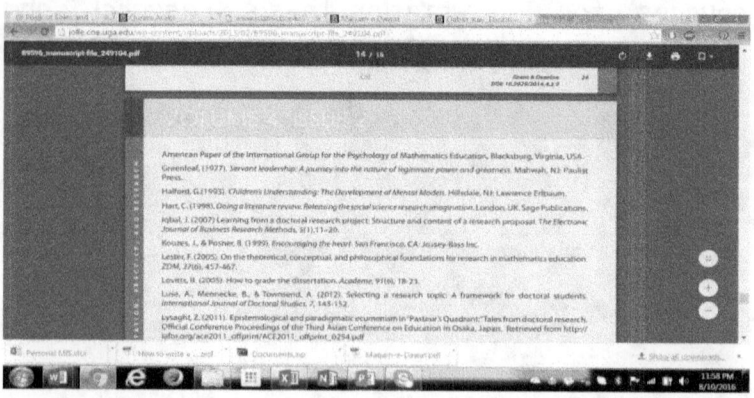

Exhibit A8

8-Google documents (Exhibit A9)

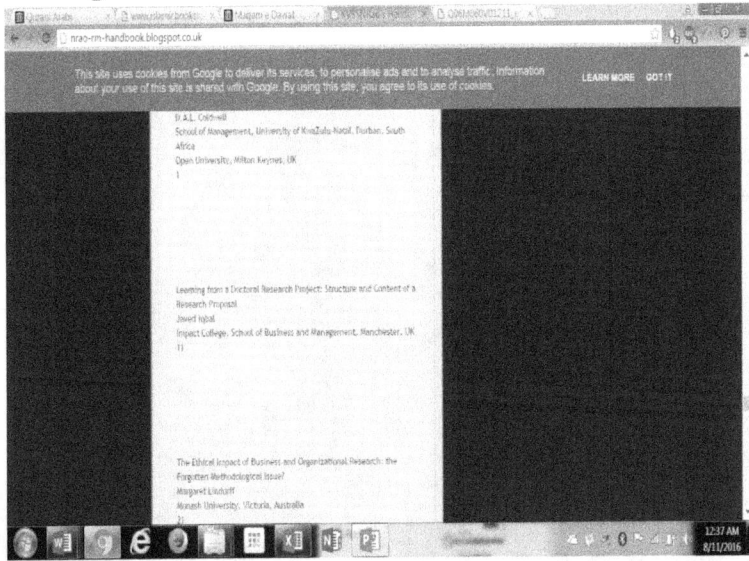

Exhibit A9

9-Handbook of Research (Exhibit A10)

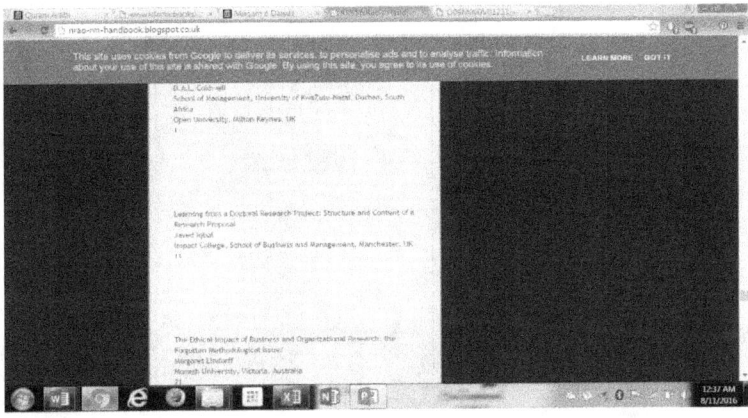

Exhibit 10

10-Military Leadership, a book (Exhibit A11)

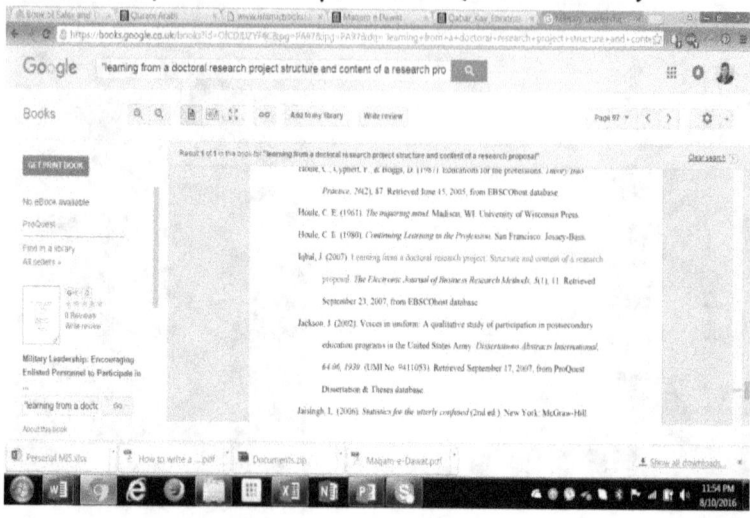

Exhibit A11

11-Scribd (Exhibit A12)

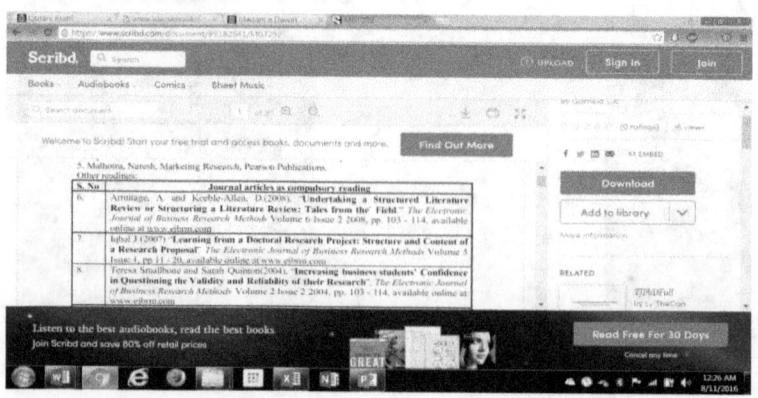

Exhibit A12

12-CiteSeerX (Exhibit A13)

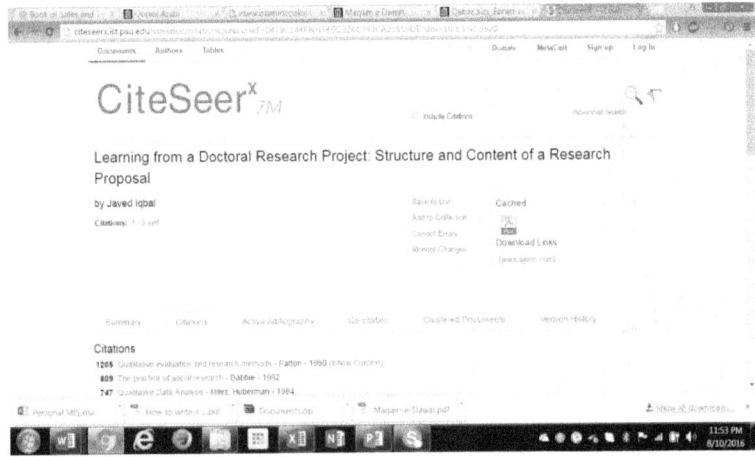

Exhibit A13

13-ISM in its list of references (Exhibit A14)

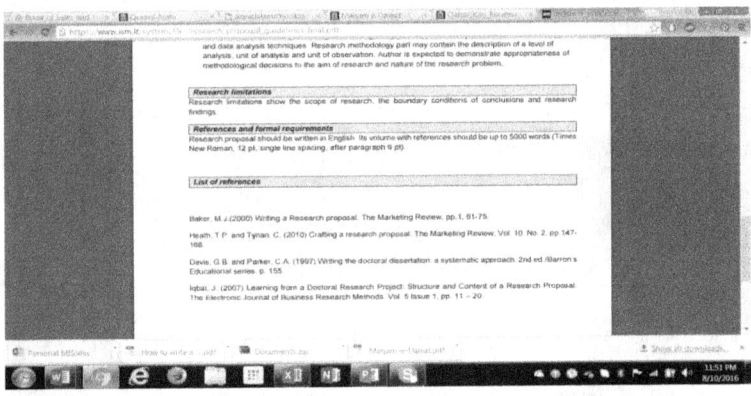

Exhibit A14

14-An article in numeristic theory (Exhibit A15)

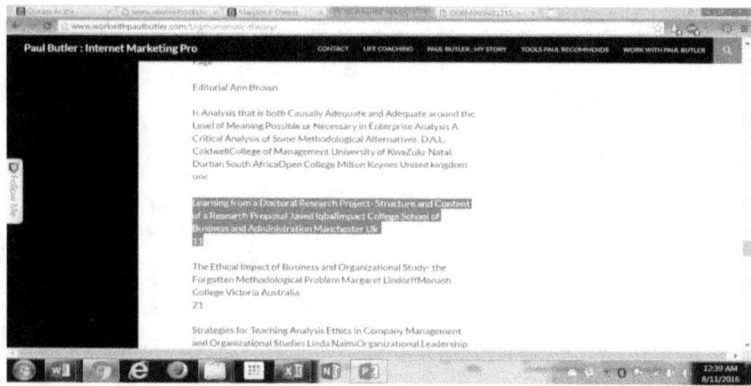

Exhibit A15

15- Mediterranean Journal of Social Sciences in the reference list of its articles (Exhibit A16)

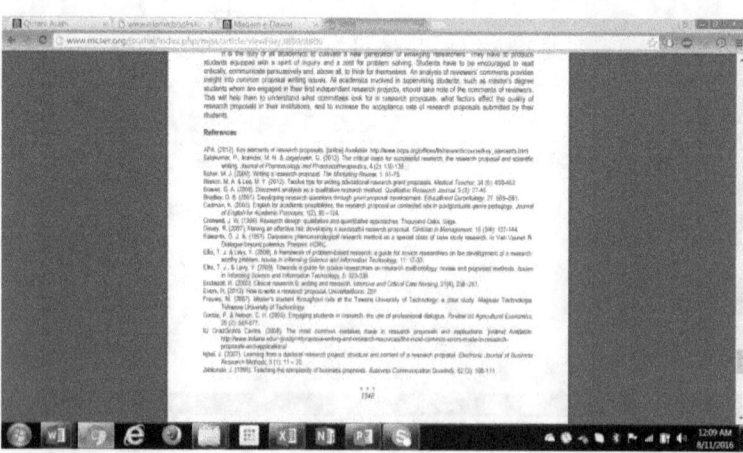

Exhibit A16

A

B

C

V

W

Y

Dr. Javed Iqbal born on 16 April 1959 in Rawalakot district Poonch Azad Kashmir. He received his early education from Pilot High School Rawalakot and received his matriculation in 1975 and intermediate from Hussain Shaheed Degree College of the same town. He earned BBA with a gold medal and an MBA with a gold medal from Azad Jammu and Kashmir University in 1986. He was appointed as a lecturer in Business Administration in the same university. Later on, he was selected by the government of Pakistan for higher studies and deputed to the United Kingdom. He received MBA from the University of Hull and Ph.D. from the University of Salford. Dr. Iqbal has been working in England in various capacities: professor, director of studies, marketing advisor and academic advisor. Dr. Iqbal returned to Home in 2006 and joined Iqra University Islamabad campus as an associate professor. He became the head of department of technology Management in International Islamic University Islamabad (IIUI). He went back to England for some time and rejoined IIUI in 2012. He joined AKU (AJ&K) as professor and Dean Faculty of Management Sciences in March 2015.

He is a distinguished teacher and world known scholar. His article title "Learning from a Doctoral Research Project: Structure and Content of a Research Proposal" has been classed by one of the professors as the best piece of knowledge for doctoral students of Deakin University in Australia. This paper is widely used and referred all over the world. Dr. Javed Iqbal has been nominated by an international organization for the Award of Distinguished Scientist for his research contribution this year. His books on various subjects are available on www.amazon.com. He poetry is to be published soon as well.

1. Iqbal, Javed Saani (2016) Responsibilities of Managers: Selected Ahadith, available on amazon.co.uk. (Paperback edition)

2. Iqbal, Javed Saani (2016) Experience: The Journey of My Life, available on amazon.co.uk. (Paperback edition)

3. Iqbal, Javed Saani (2015) Managing Projects, available on amazon.co.uk. (Paperback edition)

4. Iqbal, Javed Saani Understanding Information Systems (2012), Manchester: GRaASS.

5. Digital Divide in South Asia (2011) by Dr. Javed Iqbal, Ph.D.; ISBN: 9789699578120; available on amazon.co.uk. (Paperback edition) ASIN: B005H1OG1Q (Kindle edition)

6. Managing Risk in Projects (2011) by Dr. Javed Iqbal, Ph.D. and Muhammad Rafi Khattak; ISBN: 9789699578090; available on amazon.co.uk. (Paperback edition)

7. Understanding Project Management (2011) by Dr. Javed Iqbal, Ph.D. and Muhammad Nadeem Khan; ISBN: 978969957845; available on amazon.co.uk. ASIN: B00500JW6Y (Kindle edition)

8. Information Systems for Managers (2011) by Dr. Javed Iqbal, Ph.D.; available on amazon.co.uk. ASIN: B005YAEMPU (Kindle edition)

9. Managing strategic change: a real-world case study (2010) by Javed Iqbal, Ph.D.; ISBN: 978-3838330952, available on amazon.co.uk. (Paperback edition)

www.ingramcontent.com/pod-product-compliance
Lightning Source LLC
Chambersburg PA
CBHW070250190526
45169CB00001B/353